Lisa the Lion

by Jan Latta

Reading consultant: Susan Nations, M.Ed., author/literacy coach/consultant in literacy development

Science and curriculum consultant: Debra Voege, M.A., science and math curriculum resource teacher

GARETH**STEVENS**
PUBLISHING
A Member of the WRC Media Family of Companies

Hello! My name is Lisa, and I am a **lioness**. I live on the open grasslands of Africa with my wild animal family. Lions living in a group are called a **pride**.

3

My father has a bushy **mane**. He is strong and powerful. Some people call him the "King of Beasts."

He is bigger than my mother, and he can grow to 420 pounds (190 kilograms). My mother weighs 277 pounds (126 kg). She is about 9 feet (2.7 meters) long from her nose to the tip of her tail.

Meet my new baby brother. His name is Leon. He loves to explore, and he is very playful.

We have lots of fun together. We play and wrestle for hours. These playful fights help us practice skills that we will need for hunting. We even try to climb trees!

We keep ourselves very clean. Just like
a house cat, I lick my fur with my rough
tongue. We **groom** each other, too.

We have very good eyesight, sharp teeth, and strong jaws.

Making faces helps us smell other animals. I wrinkle my nose, lift my head, and open my mouth.

Lions like to sleep for most of the day. When we wake up, we stretch every muscle. Then it is time to hunt!

We hunt in the cool evening. My mother hides in the tall grass. The pride works together as a team. At the right moment, we can charge and pounce on our **prey**. Then we tear it apart.

Lions are **carnivores**, which means we eat meat. Male lions always eat first. Females eat next.

Cubs are the last to eat. We eat whatever food is left over. The smallest cub gets the least food.

In the morning, the pride returns home. Look what full tummies we have!

See my paw prints in the dirt? They are called **pug marks**. We have soft pads on our paws, and our claws **retract**, or pull back. When we are young, we have spots on our fur. As we grow older, the spots fade.

We **communicate** by growling and roaring. My father has the loudest roar of all. I can hear him over 5 miles (8 kilometers) away!

The total number of lions living in Africa is less than half of what it was fifty years ago. We are losing our **habitat** because people clear the land to build roads, towns, and farms.

Without help, we will not be able to live outside of zoos. Some people are learning how to protect lions. If enough people help, we might not be in danger.

Lion Facts

Did You Know?

- African lions live in large, grassy areas of land. They stay out of forests.

- Cubs are born blind.

- Cubs are usually spotted or striped.

- When cubs are four to six weeks old, their mothers introduce them to the pride.

- When cubs are three to four months old, they begin to go hunting with their mothers.

- When lions are two years old, they hunt their own prey.

- Lions will drink water every day, but they can go four or five days without it.

- Lions eat any animal they can catch.

- Lions are not great hunters. They catch fewer than half of the animals they chase.

- Female lions hunt nine times more often than male lions.

- No other animals hunt adult lions. Only humans hunt lions.

- Lions usually live ten to fifteen years in the wild. They can live up to twenty-five years in a zoo or private protected area.

- Lions are the second biggest animals in the cat family. Tigers are the biggest.

- Lions are the only big cats that form social groups.

- About twenty-three thousand lions live in Africa.

- Only about three hundred lions live in Asia. They are protected at Gir National Park in northwestern India.

- Fifteen thousand years ago, people painted lions on cave walls.

Map — Where Lions live

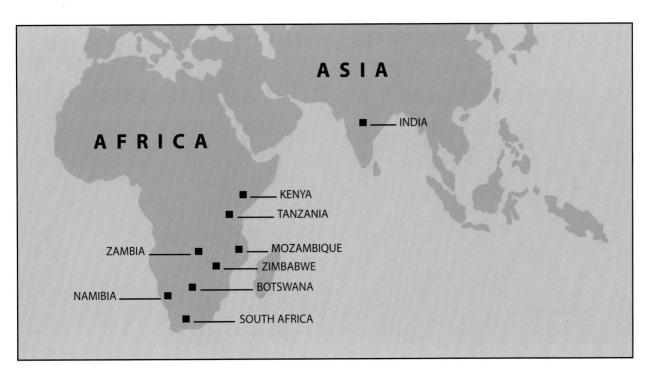

Glossary

carnivores — meat eaters

communicate — to send messages to others

groom — to lick, brush, and clean

habitat — the environment, or place, where an animal lives

lioness — a female lion

mane — a thick collar of long fur around a male lion's head

prey — the animals that are hunted

pride — a group of lions

pug marks — the foot prints of a large, wild cat

retract — to take back or pull in

More Information

Books

The Life Cycle of a Lion. The Life Cycle (series). Bobbie Kalman and Amanda Bishop (Crabtree Publishing Company)

Lions. True Books (series). Ann O. Squire (Children's Press)

Little Lions. Born to Be Wild (series). Violette Rennert (Gareth Stevens)

Web Sites

National Geographic Kids Coloring Book
www.nationalgeographic.com/coloringbook/lions.html
Color a lion picture and follow links to find out more about lions.

Smithsonian National Zoological Park: Great Cats for Kids
nationalzoo.si.edu/Animals/GreatCats/catskids.cfm
Send a post card, find fun facts, solve a lion puzzle, and more!

Publisher's note to educators and parents: Our editors have carefully reviewed these Web sites to ensure that they are suitable for children. Many Web sites change frequently, however, and we cannot guarantee that a site's future contents will continue to meet our high standards of quality and educational value. Be advised that children should be closely supervised whenever they access the Internet.

Please visit our Web site at: **www.garethstevens.com**
For a free color catalog describing Gareth Stevens Publishing's list of high-quality books and multimedia programs, call 1-800-542-2595 (USA) or 1-800-387-3178 (Canada). Gareth Stevens Publishing's fax: (414) 332-3567.

Library of Congress Cataloging-in-Publication Data

Latta, Jan.
  Lisa the lion / by Jan Latta. — North American ed.
    p. cm. — (Wild animal families)
  Includes bibliographical references.
  ISBN-13: 978-0-8368-7770-0 (lib. bdg.)
  ISBN-13: 978-0-8368-7777-9 (softcover)
  1. Lions—Juvenile literature. I. Title.
  QL737.C23L365 2007
  599.757—dc22   2006032127

This North American edition first published in 2007 by
Gareth Stevens Publishing
A Member of the WRC Media Family of Companies
330 West Olive Street, Suite 100
Milwaukee, WI 53212 USA

This U.S. edition copyright © 2007 by Gareth Stevens, Inc.
Original edition and photographs copyright © 2005 by Jan Latta.
First produced as *Adventures with Lena the Lion* by
TRUE TO LIFE BOOKS, 12b Gibson Street, Bronte, NSW 2024 Australia

Project editor: Jan Latta
Design: Jan Latta

Gareth Stevens editorial direction: Valerie J. Weber
Gareth Stevens editor: Tea Benduhn
Gareth Stevens art direction: Tammy West
Gareth Stevens Graphic designer: Scott Krall
Gareth Stevens production: Jessica Yanke and Robert Kraus

Printed in Canada

1 2 3 4 5 6 7 8 9 10 10 09 08 07 06